# My life in Africa

Michael   D M Mhike

DEDICATION

This book is dedicated to all who had gorgeous experiences in their past life, but have not reached, or are still looking for the most brilliant settlement in their future. Yet to find out that one has reached ninety years old with or without no road to settle.

# CONTENTS

# CONTENTS

# ACKNOWLEDGMENTS

I gratefully acknowledge the individuals and organisations who activated me to write this book. I will not be able to remember them all, yet I remember those whose contribution was substantial; I would like to thank the following individuals;

Anthony Bonner

Helen K Tarditi

 Lewis C Mhlanga

Tawanda L Zungunde

Wonder Duvall

# Chapter 1

## First Day at High School

Mana had finished his primary level, at the age of 13 years when he started his new boarding life at a mission high school located near a small village about eight kilometres away from his village. Mana had five brothers and one sister already betrothed now with three children, to Weston who had another wife with three children as well.

Mana was so excited to be at the boarding school to begin his secondary education as he thought it was a relief from herding cattle and goats daily as used to happen before he became a border. Now he would be able to read and sleep in a dormitory with bright lights as opposed to his village where there were no electric lights. Each time when he wanted to do the school homework, he would use candle light or even wooden light. That was stressful experience one would ever want a repeat.

He was issued school uniform as part of the high school's pre-requisites. He hoped that one day he would be able to wear shoes as he grew up. It was to his greatest fascination that his new uniform included black Kariba Shoes, as they were popularly known at this high school. It is the fact that these shoes were flat hilled with thick rim. Sports activities available were basketball, volleyball, baseball and field events like javelin, shotput, high jump, long jump, short relays and long relays on every Wednesday afternoon and Saturday mornings. He loved the indoor games but he was not good at any. To mention a few these indoor games were Chinese checkers, chess and snakes and ladders. However, this was a co-education high school so some games were co-participated with girls. In his mind, he was still searching for the favourite one where he will show his talent. He browsed all and it was evident that high jump was his capability for beating all at his school after a few months of practice and learning.

Mana had one of his brothers a teacher at the same high school. Ray taught mathematics forms 1 and 2. Ray could have offered Mana to stay with him at the teacher's quarters but decided not to. In fact, he would rather Mana stay at the dormitory with others.

Mana did not have any clue of what is going to happen in his life the next four decades. One would wish if all knew what life has had for everyone. It goes without mentioning that life can be unaccomplished sometimes.

Mana makes his first friend Sly after they both passed mock exams the second week with same percentage high mark of 98.5 percent. They spoke to each other for the first time immediately at break time and suddenly happened to be from nearby village and had both brothers' teachers, but sly brother was at another high school he would visit him whenever they were need. The high school was a co-education type so they were girls almost same number as boys.

## Chapter 2

### A Touch of Mana's childhood background stories

Mana was the last born of family of six. They were five boys and one sister. He stayed with his mother and brother Gilson at the village as all their brothers were gone to the high school boarding. His father lived at a coalmine compound doing sales for proceeds from agriculture products from the village such as groundnuts, sorghum, cane and cotton. Cotton was the chief cash crop later in the years when it was introduced. Rapoko is a cereal for fermenting traditional opaque beer.

The father would in turn send money back home used to pay school fees and purchase groceries.

There was lack of regular transport from the mine city to the village. One bus comes on every Friday once a week but would not come if they have been too much rain because the roads were gravel roads where sometimes potholes were created by erosion. Manna was very friendly to mum that he would not like to miss her unless he is going to school. His general life was sleeping up in a grass-thatched hut, which sometimes had a roof leak during rain seasons. There were children's games played at moonlight times like pada for girls and football for boys and sometimes story telling from the elders of the village. Sometimes some musicians travelled village to village playing their guitars and flutes and accordions and this was during spring times when there is not much to do in the villages. This kind of performances was done in the evenings of the moonlight days.

It was a much-needed time to come by children of the villages, as it was good entertainment for them.

Elders took this time to teach the children of the village norms and values of their society. Some of the topics included tapping talents be they story telling or dancing and leadership. The girls would learn to sing and dance while the boys would learn swimming tactics and help and work together in times of need.

There was some form of discipline and organized life in Mana's village as well as surrounding ones. There was some lack of necessary societal resources to bring comfort to the villagers. Gravel roads needed more improvement as they lead to schools, grinding mills and hospitals. They also interconnected villages for people to visit one another.

Sundays Mana would go to church as a routine. This kind of leaving was very basic; one would have wished to own a bicycle to pedal to school as the schools were a good five kilometres away. Shoes were considered a luxury if one could afford them. Mana and other children in the village did not wear shoes since birth because they were unaffordable. One borehole would serve two villages meeting at the middle because the village structure was in a straight line where fields were on one side while the paddocks were on the other and the river was an hour walk from Mana's home.

Chapter 3

**The story of the left white tennis shoe**


Mana was expecting to get some tennis shoes at the completion of his primary school. It was promised by his father that he would gladly do so if he achieves a good grade at the end of the year. This was a grade seven level. Mana studied seriously so that he could attain the highest grade. His subjects were Mathematics, General Knowledge and English.


He wrote his exams in November and the results came in early January of the following year. He retained a distinction pass mark. He could not be patient to wait to tell his father who stayed at a Mine city. Communication of those times was to tell a bus driver or conductor to deliver the message, which could also be in a written form. It would take a week to get a reply if there is not too much rain to dampen some parts of the gravel roads that the buses travelled through.


The message that he had passed grade seven with flying colours arrived at his father who was very pleased with performance of his last-born son, was such a pleasing result, the father must have thought.

Mr. Jedza was very pleased to arrange to send a pair of white tennis shoes to his boy. He was now confident that his son is going to the High school guaranteed because he had the required pass mark as was the general norms of the high school for junior schools around its district. The High school was just about eight kilometres from home as the crow flies. By road, it would be ten kilometres.

It was Saturday morning when a big parcel wrapped in a used sack arrived at Mana's home with a neighbour who had disembarked from a bus that previous night of Friday. Usual groceries were in it and Mana got his tennis shoe. Unfortunately, it was the one for the left leg and the one for the right leg could not be found. It is difficult to understand what could have happened to the right foot tennis shoe.

It was to Mana's half disappointment although he did not mind wearing just that one left shoe. He would wear it to Sunday school and he would wear it to go to herd cattle and goats. Nowadays it is funny but back in the days of Africa life Mana was a step ahead others in terms of fashion. Only the teachers and agricultural demonstrators wore shoes.

The first day he put on the white tennis shoe going to the church, other children followed him or encircle him at break to just want to touch his shoes and learn how it feels like, some children would ask to try it and he would let them do it. Mana felt great for that moment with his friends.

As news reached his father, that one tennis shoe was missing. Mana's father was a bit disturbed. He was now preparing for his next year high school fees for him. Mana's other brothers were being sponsored by missionaries but would have to pay back as soon as they started to work.

Chapter 4

## A Temporary Primary School Teacher in a remote area

It was the rule of the education ministry those days that after finishing high school one had to do at least two years practical teaching before one would be accepted to train as a qualified teacher. Mana was allocated to teach in a remote area thirty miles from the high school.

There were no buses in that area. People had to travel thirty kilometres to reach where they can catch the buses to cities and hospitals. In some cases, people had to use donkey or scotch cart to ferry ill people who need doctors' attention to the only mission general hospital in the west province of the country.

Mana is allocated to teach junior three the first year and junior four the following year at two different schools still in the same proximity. The first PTL (primary teachers lower) education school had up to grade five level of the tripartite system and the second one where he went to teach for the second year had grade seven levels.

Baobab primary school needed lot of improvements to its access roads, football and netball pitches were still under developed and in fact, it was an ongoing process. Parents were very cooperative in coming to build school for their children.

They would come every Thursday of the week to extend the buildings for more classes term to term.

Thursday is the day when villages do not go to their fields, it was a rest day, and on the same day is when the Chiefs judged all village pet crimes. In some difficult cases would then be referred to the judiciary system or police. Punishments ranged from being made a servant to the chief to being excommunicated from the village that means one had to look for residence in a different district.

By coincident Sly was also posted to teach at the same school and was taking fourth grade pupils. There was shortage of teachers as well to this area. The helping hand came from the only high school in the province, this meant that those who completed and passed high school and wanted to become teachers would be send to remote schools like Baobab to practice teaching before they can be accepted at any teacher's college in the region even countrywide.

Social standing for both Mana and Sly was great as they were first young teachers at Baobab Primary School. They were respected by the elders of the village and they owed them same. It was a good thing for Mana to be together with someone he knew. Somebody who happened to be his first friend at the high school. The two other teachers they shared with were two mature men, the Headmaster Rudd Combo teaching grade one and Ghazi Toga teaching grade five. They were all married.

 PE (physical education) was mandatory subject and had to be imparted to children on schedule. Extramural activities such as field events were also on schedule. Mana imparted Athletics skills to pupils while Sly took to impart netball and football skills every Wednesday afternoon of the week. Ghazi Toga taught music skills to pupils and the headmaster would oversee everyone. Mana and Sly always walked together after school and during weekends. They had indulged themselves into smoking a high school fever and they were quite happy to try the opaque beer made from rapoko and maize floor. It would make them spend a good weekend and socialise with local folks who were mostly peasant farmers.

.

Chapter 5

## War infection; Jecha (freedom fighters) infiltrate the Gemunu area

It was on a Friday morning time 0805minutes when the classroom door was banged open by the army infantry commander accompanied by three soldiers at gunpoint when Mana was asked to lift his hands and pupils asked to lie down on their stomachs. Mana was told to abruptly kneel on his knees, hands on top of his back head.

"Where is Jecha?" mattered, the commander dressed in army gear but his face camouflaged in black ashes smear pointing an FN rifle to Mana's forehead

"I don't know ", replied Mana trembling.

Before they could ask him a second question Mana was dragged outside like a sack and the classroom door was closed behind him. Two armed soldiers remained guarding the pupils in the classroom. Mana received a couple of beatings and punching's while outside the classroom. To his surprise, the same drama happened simultaneously to the other three teachers in other classes. Mana was raved to his teacher's quarter's room, tortured, and threatened to be shot through the head. Mana had a brother who had just visited him from abroad from a contract mine work who was also toasted but lightly compared to Mana.

The main reason for torture now was the fact that Mana like other teachers would not report the presence and were feeding the so-called terrorists who used to come at night to ask for meals and tobacco and the directions to wherever they wanted to go. It was a difficult situation for anyone in that village area to report the presence of jecha or terrorist because of the following reasons firstly the fact that they all feared for their lives as the freedom fighters threatened to kill anyone who would report them to the authorities , secondly the fact that it was a remote area where buses would come once or twice a week or never come when there is too much rainfall as roads were made of gravel and thirdly for the fact that the nearest rest camp to the police was some 30miles away, where one would run a risk of being stopped by the Jechas and be suspected to be a sell out and killed on the  way. It was a stalemate situation for everybody in the Gemunu Area. It was infested with the Jechas (children of the soil) as they always called themselves.

The headmaster was off sick that very day.

"Tell us the where they are and when they normally come to the school. "Demanded one of the soldiers.

"I better die cast, "replied now a semi unconscious Mana.

Now they were grouped together with Sly who also received some tortures.

"Your friend Sly has already agreed that he had seen the terrorists (Jecha) so tell us now the truth and we will release you "said the angry soldier pointing a 9-millimetre rifle nozzle onto Mana's head. Probably Sly had given up to beatings by agreeing to the fact that he gave them food and cigarettes.

"Just kill me", buttered Mana now pale and weak from torture.

The targeted villagers were also tortured and brought to the school assemble point and sat down in line. Pupils had been reunited with their parents at the school in this tense situation. No one was shot by the soldiers but received a considerable amount of torture. All teachers were detained except the headmaster and the school was temporary stopped for at least two months. Mana and two other teachers were detained. All parents from villages affected who took part in feeding and failing to report the presence of terrorists were detained. The rest were dismissed to go back to their respective villages. It was a dangerous phenomenon for those told to go back to their homes.

Jechas were not very far from the school, and probably they knew what was happening.

The next step was to take the three teachers and the arrested villagers with them to the spot where the Jechas used to receive food from the surrounding villagers. Food was usually delivered by single women and girls to this point, which was situated across a small tributary at a mountain peak. The peak had a good viewpoint from all directions.

Therefore, the soldiers did not give the arrested folk including Mana any guns to fight back in case crossfire was encountered. They were made to go in front in counter insurgency style. They were made to lie down talking cover from rocks since the bush towards the target area was rocky. If a missile hits a rock, then that is the end of life. The soldiers did a recognisance of the place and two freedom fighters (Jechas) were sported talking to some young girls. A missile was shot from the soldier's side and no return fire. They fired the second and the third but still no return fire, and now, a helicopter approached from a different angle blowing the huts surrounding the target, that some people were killed inside them. The advance was made to the target and no one was found there even those previously sported by the helicopter. Mana and his detainees received hash pushes and butted to move quickly as this was a live war situation. Some villagers who remained alive but were burning from their huts were uplifted by the two helicopters to the rest camp. It was Mana and his folk who did most of the first aid work as in going into the burning huts dragging the causalities to the copter. It was a tedious and dangerous event for Mana and his colleagues that day.

After no fight back happened, the mission was not completed yet. Mana and the other colleagues walked back to the school yard with the infantry soldiers to be on the same army vehicles and were whisked to the rest camp another thirty miles. As soon as they arrived at the vehicles they were chained hands and leg irons as well.

They got to the camp still with leg irons and given something to eat in a hash manner. It was at nine pm that interrogations started and this time with fresh CIDs. It was hell as each time they received big whips minute after minute. Mana saw his eyes turning red and blackout. Now, they would stop. This continued until three am the following day. After a month of tossing they were sent to remand where they met more teachers and agricultural demonstrators who had gone under the same kind of torture

All the folk were given sentences but were released because they had remained in detention for eight months as remands. Another reason was the political environment was taking a turn. Mana including all the other civil servants could go back to their respective work. It was the following year. Mana resumed teaching at a different location, which was much closer to his village cotton town.

Chapter 6

**A baby girl is born, same day of his release from Detention Remand**

It was on the 5th of April 1978 when Mana arrived home from detention. He was met in jubilation and big surprises. Only to learn that his girlfriend had just come from the local mission hospital and had a baby girl. His imagination was stuck now after learning that. It is encouraged for a boy to first make an achievement of a diploma in some discipline before one can marry. Mana was to wait for another year so that he can go to the college to complete his three-year teachers' training course. This was a stumbling block on his future. He however took it to be a father at 19years. He went to look for employment again as a temporary teacher this time near his home town so that it would be easy to monitor his family at a less travel expenses. This worked out for a while but on the third term he fetched his wife to stay with each time he went to teach at this nearby school while looking after their baby.

They were a happy couple together going back home together during school holidays and back to school. It was the last month of December when Mana was to remain at school for the whole school holiday as was his turn to do so. He also was to travel to the council about 20 miles from the school to collect cheques for other teachers as was they school routine. This would save money and time as the transport was unreliable as one would not return the same day after travelling to the council. It would be on a weekend and then return to school on either Saturday or Sunday to school and hand over other teachers' salaries on a Monday. However other teachers would visit their respective homes on the weekend to see their families. The unsettled nature had not improved on the northern part of the same district. Gorillas or freedom fighter had closed in to this new school.

As Mana's wife remained at the school yard on that weekend, she was approached and was asked about her husband's whereabouts. She told them that her husband was out on business to town but would return on Sunday night. They went into Mana's classroom and wrote political words and threatening words about the fact that they were looking for Mana. Mana arrived on Saturday evening only to find his wife trembling with fear holding their little baby girl. Mana did not waste time that evening. He packed all he could get and arranged to disappear back to his home with his little family. He dropped the cheques into the headmasters 'office and left fear of being persecuted. However, there was one week to close schools so it did not affect pupils' work as they were only waiting for the results. Mana never returned to this school again. He had his Christmas at his home which was a protected area. It means that security was present in the area and a curfew was in place.

# Chapter 7

## Mana forgets about teaching career to join the regular army

Mana couldn't do his holiday duties of remaining at the primary school to man it as he was supposed to do. He spent his Christmas at his village town. He was deciding what to do next as he had to fend his little family. Every other family member was not pleased with the acquisition of a wife as they all thought it was too early for him to be a father.

Mana 19 years old and his wife Pink 17 years of age now build their own one bedroomed house brick under thatch. They still shared the kitchen with his mother. They did field cultivation together with the mother. This was not the like of mana to do this kind of life as a means of survival. It dawns into him that he could join the army to protect himself and his family. After Christmas, he decided to visit his brother who was working a boiler maker at a national steel company based about one hundred and seventy kilometres from his home town. His brother accepted him to stay with him. Most of the day he used to just roam around the small-town suburbs to probably looks for any job for example gardener or grass cutter. It did not work out for him. He ended waiting for his brother to dismiss from work and join him when he was to go to the pub. His brother was not married at the time. He had a good senior house in the suburb well-furnished as well.

This went on for two months. Mana was caught in between situations. He couldn't go back home without finding a job whilst he couldn't return the school as the whole district was unsafe. One day he bought a local newspaper and red news that in the army they were recruiting people with previous teaching experience to become trainee cadet paymasters. Without wasting time, he asked for the fare from his brother to travel the capital where the recruiting was taking place. He got there by train the following day. He had to travel 300kilometers to the capital. When he got there only to find out that he was not alone to be interviewed. Some people came from distant cities for this job.

Everyone thought they would only be trained office work as army civilians, but it was not, everyone who passed was told that they had to do basic military training for at least six months before being trained army pay and administration course. Mana was among those who were accepted for the course. They were made to jump into an army puma vehicle and driven away for 40 kilometres from the capital. They saw soldiers in uniform everyone at this garrison camp. They were lined up to collect army jerseys and track suits and boots. They were shown a barrack to put up at night and each had a single bed and a locker. Dinner was served and they were given time to socialise and to understand what would be going on for the next six months. In fact, Mana's group was of well-educated boys and they formed a total of a platoon of 33 recruits. Every other senior soldier who were present perceived Mana's group with dignity because most were former temporary teachers and agricultural demonstrators and dip tank assistants.

However, the training process was like three little monkeys style. Hear no evil see no evil say no evil. Up and coming was a military training by what you might call crazy instructors who in themselves knew how to impact military discipline at its highest point.it was five o'clock in the morning that Mana's group was woken up and done the attestation programme and fingerprints taking. Each one had to sign the agreement to be a soldier but not sure if Mana and his group really bothered about that. They were looking forward to becoming the first paymasters in the history of their country as it was tuning to becoming independent in the near months to come. Once they were all attested they were told that they have now been welcomed into the army. They had to abide by the rules of training and had to obey their instructors. They were also told about the availability of detention barracks for those who disobey rules. This was an army CSM (company sergeant major) clad in brown skin leather with a well-shaped black stick and a leather ring on his right-hand wrist. He spoke with vigour and did not smile. Smiles went off Mana and his colleague's faces.

## Chapter 8

### Basic Military Training and deployment to the capital to take the full Pay and Administration course

The pass out parade was fascinating with other platoons from the other city being there too to do their pass out. Loads of food and beverages were prepared for this celebration. Soldiers could consume alcohol on this day which was also available. The drinking started immediately after Lunch and it was both opac beer and clear beers that every soldier drank. There was music arranged by the army band to relax everyone and to alert soldiers about what social challenges were waiting for them in future. Prayers were made to strengthen those who were going to fight in the imminent war a week to follow.

Mana and his platoon were enjoying as they looked forward to becoming first Paymasters of culture. The whole battalion was codenamed digger force. This included platoons from the other big city south of the country. Army drills of show were displayed in the early part of the morning. The summersault, assault courses, jumping of the ten-meter wall were viewed among other displays. It was a fantastic day for the whole garrison as civilian wives and children were present. Best awards were also announced.

Honour was given to Mana's platoon as they were asked to come to the front and received their label as to be the first paymasters to those who would pass the academic army funds and administration course. They were also scheduled to start training a week to follow. After this pass out parade they had to rest and return to resume their duties after five days. This time every cadet had to go and visit their parents and come back. This was done probably to let their parents understand that now they were civil servants in the form of soldiering for the country. They would also tell them that they have passed and qualified as soldiers.

This was difficult news for the parents to accept as the war was still ravaging in most parts of the country. This time every day someone was killed somewhere in the country by the freedom fighters or some places were attacked by the loyal forces and in most cases, it was the civilians.

Every platoon was deployed to different places for real-time operation facing war except Mana and the platoon because they were going to the offices to start their academic training as was advertised before they knew they were going to start military training first.

This was a life changer environment for Mana and his colleagues. They were no longer working up at five to start running and assault course exercises, in fact they are now working up at seven in the morning for breakfast in a mess where food was served by qualified chefs and the food was first class. In the lecture room they learnt about administration, pay and records of every soldier in the country. A test had to come after six weeks and Mana passed it and was further deployed to a midland city to start as a pay clerk for the next six months. Mana was working with a team of four him being the fifth.it took him a couple of days and months to do the practical work and understanding it. It was not easy course though yet manna worked hard to pass it because this was another huddle before he could apply to be considered for an officers training course.

In the meantime, Life after work for Mana was great because they were allocated better houses in a suburban area. Mana got respect as gold finger from other soldiers of neighbouring army camps as well as the city dwellers. He leaved a better life and acquired friends of high dignity even though he had not been an officer yet. This is because the office was every soldiers' destination each month end.

Mana was involved in a taxi driver's scam when he failed to pay the full fare because he was so drunk that he couldn't remember his name. The taxi driver left him but remembered his office of work. The girlfriend he had told the taxi driver of Mana's workplace as she also had no money to pay the driver. This was on a late Sunday evening from a binge drinking in the city. He leaved ten kilometres away from the city.

On Monday at ten o'clock a phone arrived from the taxi driver to the chief paymaster in the same office with Mana. The message was that Mana from that office had failed to pay the fare on that previous Sunday night. The Chief Paymaster asked Mana to pay his due and he immediately went to the bank and paid the taxi driver but that left Mana with a bad record to the Chief Paymaster.

After six weeks Mana received an offer to go to the army headquarters to train as a Paymaster.

## Chapter 9

### Syndicate 25 of the 150 Syndicates, passes

Mana had to return to the capital to sit an officer selection course. This time there was an on-going situation in his country of attesting ex freedom fighters into the army. Therefore, it meant the officer selection included some nominated freedom fighters that were themselves divided. Mana belonged to the former forces that were fighting against these freedom fighters before independence in sometime in the first quarter of the year.

The total number of those selected came to 150 candidates. The selection process took two weeks and it ran from eight o'clock in the morning to five o'clock in the afternoon with one-hour lunch break and thirty minutes' tea break each day of the training period. The syndicates of ten groups that mean they were 15 in each syndicate group. The testing panels were ten and formed of brigadiers and army protocol staff. There was a big hall in the officer's mess which was used to brief battalion commanders and this was the one for debrief to the officer cadets.

"My name is Brigadier Son, so I am here to monitor the selection process, and will be with you throughout the whole selection process which shall take two weeks. Those who succeed after two weeks would be given green boards to wear on their shoulder for a further six weeks period where they will be groomed on the social aspects side of officers' life', he carried on... clad in his service medals and brigadier ranks onto his shoulders,' I believe you all want to become the pay officers in the army, and I wish you all the best", he said, there was moment of silence perhaps an applause would have been most suitable but not at this time because it was only the beginning.

He introduced his judges being the testing panel composed of five dignitaries in a group of ten.

There were ten bridges to cross each day of the selection process. It was a tense situation for Mana. He had to pull up his socks to complete the tasks required.

Each testing panel had a different questions and tasks from each other and their art changed daily. Questions asked for an example were what a man is and could you talk five minutes about anything, could be paper, grass etc. Maths IQs and general knowledge IQs were among the rest. Mana had little difficulties in answering some of the questions because of his previous teaching experience. Some candidates surrendered even before completing the selection. At the end of the selection, only 125 could complete the course but did not all pass.

The fourteenth day arrived and results of the course were based on individual performances. How one has managed to convince the all ten members of the panel, judges so to speak, or has won most the judges. It was a difficult situation to imagine for everyone involved in the selection.

It was announced that only thirty-three members have managed to go through but would be told individually. Mana was called into an office of high profile army figures. They asked Mana's name. They waited for a moment considering Mana's face. Perhaps to see if Mana has a state of confusion, of-course Mana was in that state. One said Mana you have passed the officer selection course and from now you are a Green Board Officer and you will be allocated a region where you shall be responsible for pay and records of the army personnel in that region and Good luck!" exclaimed the high-profile man who pronounced the results.

Mana saluted as was always the case and step back and about turned in the right army fashion style and filled with joy he waited outside to wait his colleague who appeared in twenty minutes with a brighter face. They celebrated that evening in the officer's mess, as this was their first time to mess there, as there shall always be.

.

# Chapter 10

## Gold Finger Midlands Region, to Pay and administer four battalions

The pay office was the someone which he used to work as a pay clerk. He arrived with his pay team colour sergeant, full corporal, and two private soldiers. The outgoing paymaster was in the office to do the hand over and take over procedures. These were done while the other staff were busy compiling acquittance rolls. The colour sergeant was going through the telegrams to see if they were any status changes with any recorded payees. He would check any transfers, marriages and notices as these affect payee's salary process.

This regiment was termed the Tenth-Regiment.

It was run by adjutant Commander Car McMillon. He did the administration of the regiment which comprised of the head mechanic who took care of the army vehicles that needed repair with his staff, head of the Regimental Police who manned the place and his boys, the chef who took care of the canteen and the quartermaster who issued uniforms for the soldiers. They were no barracks at the regiment but were available at the military academy situated about a mile away. This was probably because the regiment was situated very much in the city. After working hours' corps had to leave for their barracks and some went to their suburban house if they were married.

Mana had to sign for a vehicle it was a land rover series 2, and would be accompanied by the driver, two staff at the back of the car with their riffles loaded just in case of robbers. He arrived at the bank vault and security was there waiting for his team. This was a cash run for the first time in the lead. Two black army trunks were loaded with all to pay the battalions in the midlands regions. Totalling to about two point five million dollars. It was not an easy job this time because Mana had to count every penny up to two point five million. It took him and the senior bank tailor one and half hours to satisfactorily count and receive the money. It was locked in the trunk and he retained the keys and drove back to the regiment to start to prepare for payment commencing the following day. This involved cash breakdown to suit each a quittance roll for every battalion. The following morning a battalion paying officers would arrive the office to collect payroll sheets and money already prepared for him but not put in individual envelopes. He would pay soldiers in cash at hand.

Mana and his team finished at nearly midnight counting and allocating funds to ten battalions. Bac system was not introduced this time. Mana had to retire to the hotel as would be always the case. It was not very bad experience for Mana at least there was a mixture of work and social life. His team were also booked at a different hotel.

There was not much time to sleep as he would be required to report to the regiment at half seven in the morning for duty. They paid all the battalion paying officers the whole day in the same manner Mana received the money from the bank. This took them up to five in the evening. This was not the end of the paying process. Manna would wait five working days for the paying officers to pay and return the signed pay rolls. The reason is that some battalions were as far as a hundred miles away.

In total number of days Mana and his team would stay for two weeks and would be back on the train again to the headquarters after balancing books. He would make a report of the whole transaction and timing scale. At the Headquarters Mana and his team would net into the other team and start deal with salary queries and debit balances for his midlands region. It was quite some challenging job for Mana yet he enjoyed it.

Mana had an apartment in the officer's mess where he lived as he was a single officer. Sometimes he would go to his girlfriend's house who lived in the city avenues after work as he used to drive a 1300 alfa Romeo car.

Mana worked for three years as a regional paymaster and reposted to become the input section officer after the introduction of army and air force data processing computer systems or code named ADPU (Army Data Processing Unit). This was in the capital as well, two miles from the Army Headquarters.

## Chapter 11

### Input Section Officer at Army Headquarters

The section was comprised of all paying units for various army departments in the country. His main job was to rectify and input the pay records, and deal with staff promotions and welfare. Now, he was appointed Section Officer Commanding. He was promoted as a Captain.

Daily, he had to deliver the pay records to another department situated in the city some mile away. He had to do this usually after lunchtime when every unit has submitted the necessary documents and he would have checked and approved them for pay changes for the next month. What affected the soldier's income were promotions, living out allowances, travel and subsistence and reports from regional paymasters. They had to appear on the next salary.

According to Mana this was challenging job. No mistakes were allowed and correct timing was required. He enjoyed his new job. Mana was reporting directly to the Chief of Staff of Pay Corps situated in the Army Commanders Department a separate building from his team's floor.

He did this for almost a year and something was not pleasant each time he joined other officers in the officer's mess for his dinner. His country had just attained independence about two years back. Officers were divided into four groups and so were the dinner tables. The four groups were comprised of two former freedom fighters group which had their former vendetta from the bush and two groups separated by colour who wants worked together before former fighters were attested into the army but would no longer sit together at the dinner table because of the majority colour with the former freedom fighters but would not share a dinner table. These four camps were like a timing bomb. Mana could feel the heat going into the dining room. They shared no information with each other except to say good morning or evening. No one could make changes to this kind of a somewhat tense situation. Even distribution of ranks was not fair. Only those coming from the bush had the privilege of being promoted quick and even housing loans, it was in the same manner. Manna tried a loan for mortgage but couldn't get it. The Chief of Staff members were former freedom fighters so it was like a dragon's den.

Mana thought of this for a while and it affected him and he decide to leave the army. It took him three months to receive his approval to resign. Mana had earmarked another job at local airport to work as bar uplift manager. He got the job within three months of his resignation. It has always been hard feelings to join the civics world as there is a vast difference in thinking between a civilian and a properly trained soldier. For example, a soldier has a formulated opinion whilst a civilian has various opinion.

Mana worked for nine months and joined the national airline as a Purser. It was a thriller job to him as it was scary to fly for the first time yet it was a cracker to visit other countries he had never thought he would in his life time. The new job was interesting as it involved talking to people of other countries and of other cultures. He made friends from his country and from abroad.

This was a turn of events of his lifetime. He made a good life of himself and he married and had two children. Every time he went on holidays he used to take his family abroad say about once a year. He did many diplomas during his spare time and he encouraged his wife to upgrade her education and she achieved a private secretary diploma and their children went to preschool. Mana also achieved a ten-year loyalty award with the IATA Arline he worked for. After 14 years of service a redundant scheme was offered and Mana and 400 others opted for it and were given their Package together with travel packs for life. Two years towards redundant scheme Mana had family problems as their love was on the rocks. They had to separate and divorced.

Chapter 12

**An Investment Company, starts with a Computer Academy for the local community in the capital**

Mana had premediated that one day he would become a business man helping the community on how to qualify for regional and national travel using the airline mode of travel and enhancing computer skills. Mana had done his homework before he opted for the redundant scheme. He was faced with staffing challenge for his new company. He registered an investment company to deal with impacting computer skills, travel and tourism.

It was early morning of the first day after his voluntary resignation from the airline that he walked into his office situated at a shopping mall in the area he lived. The first thing was to set up the designer of his new office and to fill it with the necessary furniture and equipment. In this office, he set up a computer academy which he started with four computers. One computer would be at the reception and the other three were used to engage three leaners who were taught and manned by one qualified teacher. Two staff were in this office, one a secretary would type documents for community people of a nature, and the other a teacher who would teach computer beginners. Mana had to be busy adverting his business by going to the national newspaper to pay for the services. He would constantly go to the office to solve any issues that could need his attention and he sat for an hour twice each day.

This was a great experience for Mana as this time he would be the sole decision maker to the way he would like his business to take direction. He was aware of the great completion around him in the capital. However, the advantage Mana had, was that he had broader knowledge about this business from his previous work where he had worked for almost 15 years. His business became popular and Mana had customers from greater areas of the capital. Many were trained at his computer academy.

Within six months there was so much demand of his services for the community that Mana Had to reconsider how to accommodate clients. He clinched a deal with the local church to get extra room to serve his students. He had to employ two extra qualified teachers who had diplomas and degrees in computer packages. His records revealed that his academy had reached a record high of one hundred and fifty students within three months later. It was a multiracial computer academy and he got a good feedback from the local councillors for bringing such innovation into the community.

Mana delved into guest houses by renting a full seven bedroomed house in the same community. This location was ideal because it was not far from the international airport he once was working at and its locality was middleclass. The suburban house was on a five acre plot adjacent to a busy road, twin pines at the entrance gate. He nicknamed the Twin Pines Guest house because of this. He created a twenty cars park lanes for his guests. He designed a stylish bar which was breath-taking to every guest who entered. A housekeeper, laundry person and three barmen were hosted after an induction course done at his academy. Guests from all over the planet were clients at his guest house. There was great experience for Mana although he enjoyed doing this job while working for the national airline.

A setback came when the owner of the house gave notice to take it back in a months' notice. Mana bought a resort area near a five-square kilometre man made dam. It took him three months to complete and renovating some structures while he was reassuring his clients that he was designing good resort area with extra benefits for example opportunity to fishing yachts, gazebos and spar.

The resort was complete and business as usual. three months down the line a political wave struck the country and it looked not secure any more to run the business especially when the currency started to plummet against other major currencies. What was the next thing to do again in this African region? Mana decides to relocate his business to his local village. He did so within four months.

He sold his academy, his resort and proceeded to his village town to start a travel shop and a commodity broking enterprise. It took him six months to rebuild his business. He dealt with travel tour packages and taking trips to overseas to meet business counterparts.

Even though Mana prospered again in his village town the unsettled nature of his country paved its way.it divided people into political parties and it was difficult to show which part one would support.one had to do it discreetly, and most eyed were people running businesses. This became a worry to Mana. It was a tough situation to be in. However, Mana had his uncle active in the opposition party so he decides to sign checks towards the party a donation and would be discreetly be sent to his uncle. If discovered the consequences would be lethal for Mana's life. It was in the silent moment of Mana's personal and private life that his greatest dreams were no more. He felt as if he was in the road to Neverland.

While on his overseas trip he had a phone call from his secretary that his office was ransacked by the other political party and staff had to leave if they wanted to survive. Mana would not return home fear of persecution yet he had no choice except to seek asylum in that overseas country he first visited. Is this his noblest dreams come to an end or true or compensation for what he has been through?

Mana felt that he had run out of gold from his own country. It is where he was born but cannot go, it is where he knew people he grew up with but can he go back? if so after so many yes would he be able to pick up pace with his counterparts? Mana is leaving in two worlds of the planet and his age for implementing business plans seems to meander. He is just hoping that one day he would be able to see his scattered family tree all in Africa.

## ABOUT THE AUTHOR

Michael Mhike was born in Zimbabwe in 1958 .He achieved some disciplines in IATA(International Air Transport Association) Hague 1990,Tourism and Travel Agency Management at New Jersey Channel Islands 1991 , a certificate of transport management and fleet control with Zimbabwe Traffic Safety board 1988 and Marketing certificate(Bulawayo Polytechnic 1994) majoring in Customer Service Strategies , Public Relations and Selling Techniques also attained a 10 years loyalty certificate with his National Airline air Zimbabwe in 1985.
Michael Mhike has helped imparting computer skills to students in his local suburb Hatfield   based in Harare through his computer academy at Kilwinning shopping mall. He also opened travel shop in Sanyati town which helped community to learn about travelling abroad.
Michael Mhike travelled to settle in the United Kingdom where he became a local councilor for Mary hill District Council 2009/13 and nominated an executive member of Mary hill Integration Network (2011/14 which helps integrate people. He has also achieved some business studies at stow college and is to complete his IT networking course at Anne island college in Glasgow.
He has four children in Africa and lives in The Central Lowlands of Scotland.

Printed in Great Britain
by Amazon